Old DALRY in EDINBURGH

by
Malcolm Cant

A sea of expectant faces, part of the huge workforce of men and women employed by the North British Rubber Company at Castle Mills off Dundee Street. The company produced a vast range of products including rubber boots and shoes, motor car tyres, conveyor belts, combs, hot water bottles and golf balls.

© Malcolm Cant 2002
First published in the United Kingdom, 2002,
by Stenlake Publishing
Telephone / Fax: 01290 551122

ISBN 1 84033 211 5

THE PUBLISHERS REGRET THAT THEY CANNOT SUPPLY COPIES OF ANY PICTURES FEATURED IN THIS BOOK.

ACKNOWLEDGEMENTS

I would like to acknowledge the assistance of the following people or organisations in lending material (in some cases several years ago) and providing information which has now been used and has greatly enhanced this book: Adult Learning Project; Better Gorgie Dalry Campaign; Alan Brotchie; Caledonian Distillery archive; Dalry Primary School; Mrs H. O. Duncan; Edinburgh & Leith Age Concern; Bill Forrest; Robert Grieves; Tommy Jamieson; Colin Macandrew & Partners Ltd.; Mrs Jean McCran; Bill McKenzie; Revd Stewart McPherson; Mrs Ruth Mather; Peter Miller; Mrs Lottie Morrice; James Murie; Orwell Primary School; Royal Commission on the Ancient & Historical Monuments of Scotland; St Martin's Episcopal Church; Tom Scott; Scottish National Portrait Gallery; Mrs Pat Scoular; Mary Wilson.

The publishers would like to thank Jack Stasiak for allowing the use of his pictures of the North British Rubber Company.

Dalry Road railway junction lay on the Caledonian line out of Princes Street station between the south side of Caledonian Crescent and the north side of Dundee Street. Here the train is on the main line running west to Merchiston and Slateford stations. To the left of the picture a branch line led to Dalry station on the Granton line. There were also separate tracks to the maintenance area known as Dalry sheds, separated from Dalry cemetery by the aptly named Coffin Lane.

INTRODUCTION

In 1995 I wrote and published a book called *Edinburgh: Gorgie and Dalry*. As this is now almost out of print I was very pleased to be asked by Stenlake Publishing to put together two photographic records of the districts under the titles *Old Dalry* and *Old Gorgie*. When I first researched these areas some years ago now, I gathered a large number of photographs, many of which were never used in the original book. This new publication now gives the opportunity to use these photographs, along with some of the others. The boundary between Gorgie and Dalry has been taken as the Ardmillan junction, but some difficulty has been encountered in allocating pictures in and around Murieston. All I can say is that if your favourite view is not in *Old Dalry* perhaps it will be in *Old Gorgie*.

Old Dalry covers the area from Haymarket to Ardmillan Terrace including the many side streets en route. Historically, the lands of Dalry stretched as far south as the roads now known as Fountainbridge and Dundee Street, which has given me the chance to include a few excellent photographs of the former North British Rubber Co. Ltd., whose extensive works lay between Fountainbridge and the Union Canal.

The modern district of Dalry has developed over many years from its origins as a quiet, rural backwater near the metropolis of Edinburgh. Nevertheless, much of that rural character was still evident up until the last quarter of the nineteenth century. The lands of Dalry stretched from Semple Street, near Tollcross on the east side, to the boundary with the lands of Gorgie on the west side. From the mid-seventeenth century the dominant centre of influence was Dalry House, situated about midway between the east and west boundaries, and, to a lesser extent, Easter Dalry House, in what is now Distillery Lane, near Haymarket. As late as the 1860s Dalry House was still surrounded by its own grounds with two access driveways from Dalry Lane (now Dalry Road). A third driveway from Fountainbridge crossed the line of the Caledonian Railway (now the West Approach Road) and entered the estate grounds from the south. Little evidence of the estate remains today, but Dalry House survives in Orwell Place, hemmed in on all sides by tenement buildings of the late nineteenth century. The way in which this transformation took place is the story of Dalry.

Dalry House dates from 1661 but the surrounding estate can be dated to at least the fourteenth century. In the eighteenth century the house and estate were sold separately, which meant that the owner of the house and its immediate policies did not have control over how the wider estate was developed. One of the greatest changes was the coming of the railways which was probably the biggest single factor in prompting further development. The Edinburgh & Glasgow line was opened to Haymarket station in 1842 and the Caledonian line was opened to Princes Street station in 1848. One of the first industries to take advantage of the new transport links and the greenfield sites was the Caledonian Distillery, which moved into its Haymarket site in 1855. Many more industries followed, requiring a substantial workforce. By the last quarter of the nineteenth century Dalry, and later Gorgie, were firmly established as Edinburgh's centres of industry, second only to Leith.

The main build-up in the population of Dalry occurred in the latter part of the nineteenth century, notably from the mid-1860s. Sporadic development began along the north side of what is now Dalry Road, nearest to Haymarket, no doubt influenced by the arrival of the Caledonian Distillery. By 1868 the terraces on the south side of Dalry Road were under construction and the last remnants of the Dalry House policies were earmarked for the streets around Caledonian Crescent. The houses in and around Murieston Road were completed around 1888 but for reasons which are not now known parts of Cathcart Place, Springwell Place and Downfield Place were not completed until the late 1880s. The mason's progress in Downfield Place is recorded on date stones on the face of the tenement: 1887 at Nos. 17, 20 and 22; 1888 at No. 12; and 1903 at No. 26. Census returns between 1851 and 1891 show how the population altered from mainly groups of families in fairly isolated farms and cottages to the greater density of tenement life. In the process, of course, the occupations also changed from farm workers to railway workers, brewers and the like. Many of the tenement houses had only two rooms for six or more occupants, and by present-day standards the facilities were very basic. A high percentage of adults listed in the census returns were born outside Edinburgh, suggesting that the new industries were attracting people from other parts of Scotland. As the population grew, schools, churches and places of entertainment were built.

During the First and Second World Wars, many firms in Dalry turned their attention to the manufacture of items required for the war effort, but some years after 1945 the district fell into a long period of partial decline, not seriously halted until the 1980s when organisations such as the Better Gorgie Dalry Campaign were established 'to promote, develop and sustain the economic and physical regeneration of the Gorgie Dalry area'. A lot has been achieved and there is still room for new ideas, especially as Edinburgh's new financial centre at Morrison Street continues to creep towards Haymarket.

Dalry House in Orwell Place dates from 1661. The year, and various insignia, are incorporated in the ceiling plasterwork in one of the principal rooms on the first floor. Originally the house was a simple Z-plan structure of three storeys, standing in an extensive estate which stretched from Semple Street on the east side to the boundary with Gorgie on the west, and from Dalry Road on the north to Dundee Street on the south side. The house was built more than two centuries before the tenement buildings which now surround it, and was extended and improved on numerous occasions: in the early eighteenth century an extension was built to the north; around 1800 a similar extension was added to the south; in 1877 school accommodation was built by John Watherston & Sons; and in 1965 extensive modernisation and improvement was carried out under the direction of architects Robert Hurd & Partners. Dalry House was probably built by Walter Chieslie whose family owned the entire estate, including Easter Dalry House (situated in what is now Distillery Lane). Chieslie did much to improve the lands of Dalry in the seventeenth century. However, that sense of duty was not inherited by his son, John, who had a wife, ten children and various marital problems which eventually led him to appear in court to answer a claim for alimony. The evidence was heard by Lord President Lockhart in the Court of Session who awarded the sum of £93. John Chieslie was so incensed by the judgement that he lost all reason and threatened to kill the Lord President. Unfortunately for all concerned he was as good as his word. On Easter Sunday, 31 March 1689, he lay in wait for the Lord President as he made his way from St Giles' Cathedral to his house in Old Bank Close and brought him to the ground with a single fatal shot. The unremorseful Chieslie was apprehended, tried and sentenced to death. Before the execution his right hand was cut off and the pistol used in the crime hung around his neck. The exact place of execution is in doubt but it is said that Chieslie's supporters recovered the body and brought it back to Dalry House, which was thereafter haunted by a shadowy figure which glided between the house and a recess in the garden wall. Many years later, when the wall was being repaired, the skeleton of a man was found – complete in every detail save the right hand!

The Walker family lived at Dalry House longer than any other family and hung on to their mansion until it was completely surrounded by industrial development and tenement buildings. The first James Walker bought part of the estate in 1790 and a second portion plus the mansion in 1812. He was succeeded by the second and third James Walkers who saw the estate greatly altered, firstly by the construction of the Union Canal in 1822 and then the arrival of the Caledonian Railway in 1848. In the early 1870s the Walker family sold Dalry House to the Scottish Episcopal Church to be used as a training college for teachers, and in 1963 the church gifted the building to the Edinburgh & Leith Old People's Welfare Council. As seen in this photograph, an appeal was launched to raise £50,000 for renovations. This had gathered £100,000 by the time the building was opened by Her Majesty the Queen on 17 October 1967. Part of the restoration work included harling and painting the outside of the building, covering up the bare stonework seen here.

When Dalry House opened in 1967 it was run as a day centre and lunch club for the elderly by Edinburgh & Leith Old People's Welfare Council, whose principal aim was 'to promote and assist in the welfare of elderly people in Edinburgh and its environs'. It organised a varied programme of activities for men and women including swimming, dancing, bingo, handicrafts, cooking and musical entertainment. Several special events were arranged at Dalry House in 1992 to celebrate its silver jubilee, including an open day on 4 September.

In recent years the Edinburgh & Leith Old People's Welfare Council has changed its name to Edinburgh & Leith Age Concern (ELAC). One of the most popular classes at the present day is Computer Training for the 50+, which offers the chance to gain skills in word-processing and the use of the internet. These two photographs illustrate how Edinburgh & Leith Age Concern has changed with the times without losing sight of its original aims. The upper photograph shows the ladies' sewing group in 1967, and the lower one the painting group in 2002.

Fountain House, the last of the grand houses of Fountainbridge, was demolished in 1934. It stood on the north side of Dundee Street slightly to the east of the junction with Viewforth, on ground which now belongs to Scottish & Newcastle's Fountain Brewery. This well-proportioned building of three storeys plus basement is of uncertain date, but was probably built shortly after 1763 when the ground on which it stood was feued by William Kirkpatrick of Dalry House to Alexander Bain. The house was later acquired by the Gardner family who owned it until 1862 when the family's last surviving daughter died. Fountain House was subsequently acquired by J. & B. Greig, the engineers, and this photograph was taken shortly before its demolition in 1934. The large gate pillars on the left mark the original south entrance to Dalry House. Here the original gates have been replaced with timber doors with an inset entry typical of the style used in industrial properties.

St Martin of Tours Episcopal Church, *c*.1905. John Robertson's French Gothic design in red and white stone was a prominent landmark on the corner of Gorgie Road and Murieston Road from 1900 until the early 1980s when the church was demolished. The foundation stone was laid on 15 July 1899 and the first service was held on 14 July 1900. Robertson drew up very detailed and intricate plans, and comprehensive schedules (which still survive in West Register House in Edinburgh) were put together for the various tradesmen to quote costs. However, despite this careful planning all did not go according to plan. A shortage of money meant that the intended seven-bay nave was shortened to four bays and the proposed grand tower and steeple, on the south-east corner, was stopped below the level of the main roof. At a later date a brick chancel was grafted onto the north end of the truncated nave but the bond was not a happy one. Nave and chancel went their separate ways, opening up a dangerous gap between the two structures which eventually led to their demolition around 1983. Undeterred, but obviously disappointed at the loss of their church, St Martin's congregation moved a few hundred yards east to the building vacated by the Baptist Church on the corner of Dalry Road and Murieston Crescent. The pipe organ, reredos and lectern were all transferred from the old building and refitted in the new place of worship.

St Martin's Football Club 1931–32. There is no record of this cup-winning team being a serious threat to their immediate neighbour, the Heart of Midlothian Football Club.

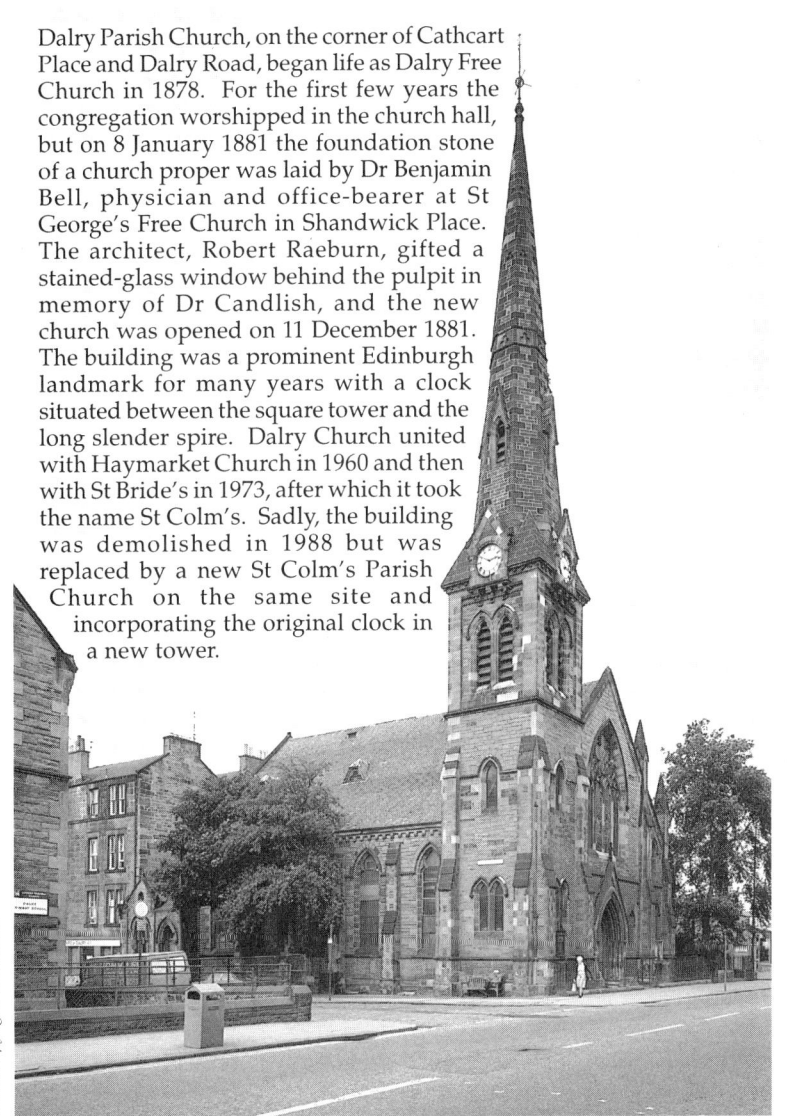

Dalry Parish Church, on the corner of Cathcart Place and Dalry Road, began life as Dalry Free Church in 1878. For the first few years the congregation worshipped in the church hall, but on 8 January 1881 the foundation stone of a church proper was laid by Dr Benjamin Bell, physician and office-bearer at St George's Free Church in Shandwick Place. The architect, Robert Raeburn, gifted a stained-glass window behind the pulpit in memory of Dr Candlish, and the new church was opened on 11 December 1881. The building was a prominent Edinburgh landmark for many years with a clock situated between the square tower and the long slender spire. Dalry Church united with Haymarket Church in 1960 and then with St Bride's in 1973, after which it took the name St Colm's. Sadly, the building was demolished in 1988 but was replaced by a new St Colm's Parish Church on the same site and incorporating the original clock in a new tower.

This distinctive building was the church hall for Dalry Church until its demolition in 1988. When Dalry Free Church was established it was financed by its parent church, St George's Free in Shandwick Place, which paid for the construction of the hall in which services were held at first. By the early 1920s the hall accommodation was badly in need of upgrading. To finance an extension, a bazaar was held in the Music Hall in George Street (now the Assembly Rooms) in December 1924 which raised over £3,000. Among the many entertainments offered, one, at least, no longer has current appeal: 'the Electric Coil – one penny per shock'. With the money raised, the congregation proceeded to take the roof off the old hall, jacked it up by twelve feet, inserted a new floor and heightened the walls to the new position of the roof. In this way they created a two-storey building with a separate hall on each level.

The first Dalry School occupied very small premises in Washington Lane, off Dalry Road, from 1875 to 1878. A much bigger school on the corner of Cathcart Place and Dalry Road (seen here) was opened under the auspices of the Edinburgh School Board on 18 February 1878. By 1897 the roll had reached 1,884 pupils which put considerable strain on the accommodation and the resources of the staff. In 1889 the headmaster, Mr Martin, earned £410 per annum; his first assistant was paid less than half of that at £175. The infant mistress earned £192 and the teachers received between £65 and £120 per annum depending upon their experience. Evidence of inequality between the sexes was not hard to find: male pupil-teachers were paid just over £17 per annum and female pupil-teachers just over £12 during their first year of apprenticeship. Fees were also charged: infants paid 2*d*. per week; juveniles paid up to 7*d*. per week depending upon their age; and the Parochial Boards paid a standard amount of 4*d*. per week for each child whose parents could not afford to pay. When fees were outstanding the headmaster asked the janitor to call to see the parents and investigate the reasons for non-payment.

A class of nine-year-olds (20 boys and 30 girls) photographed in 1932 with their teacher, Miss Green, at the Normal Practising School in Orwell Place. The Episcopal Training College for teachers was established in Dalry House around 1877 and in 1881 the Episcopal Church opened the Edinburgh Episcopal Normal School in the adjacent building to the south. According to the school log book for 16 May 1975 the head teacher of the day asked that the name of the school be changed because 'the old name . . . was proving to be an embarrassment to both staff and pupils'. After 1975 the school was renamed Orwell Primary School, although many former pupils were sorry to see the old name disappear.

Colin Macandrew & Partners Ltd. had their offices and workshops at West End Place between 1919 and 1967. A siding from the Caledonian Railway gave access to the yard for bringing in materials and taking away finished work. Prior to the First World War, Macandrew was the main contractor on several important public buildings in Edinburgh including Morningside Free Church (now Church Hill Theatre), designed in 1892 by Hippolyte Blanc; the Royal Infirmary of Edinburgh Diamond Jubilee Pavilion (1897); and, perhaps the biggest contract ever undertaken by Macandrew, Redford Barracks, begun in 1909. Before work was started on the barracks, a light railway was built from Slateford station to Colinton Road to transport the vast quantity of stone, timber and other materials required for the job. Between 1918 and 1939 several other important Edinburgh buildings were completed, including George Heriot's Junior School, George Watson's Junior School and the Princess Margaret Rose Hospital. Perhaps the most prestigious of all, however, was the National Library of Scotland on George IV Bridge, designed in 1934 but delayed by the outbreak of the Second World War and not completed until 1955.

A group of stonemasons employed by Macandrew photographed at West End Place, probably in the 1920s. The working week, as with most other trades of the period, was 44 hours – 8.00 a.m. to 4.30 p.m. Monday to Friday with half an hour for lunch, and 8.00 a.m. to 12 noon on Saturday. Apprentices were given a thorough training but were also expected to do the menial tasks such as 'biling the cans' – old 2 lb. syrup tins with the rim cut off and a wire handle added which the men used as a practical alternative to cups.

New in 1920, SG 761 was a W. & G. lorry, manufactured in Acton, London by W. & G. Ducros Ltd., a well-known operator of London taxi-cabs prior to World War I. A number of buses were also built in the 1920s by this company, some of which ran in Scotland. Here the lorry is being used by Macandrew's men to move heavy stones.

Around the same time, in the 1920s, the same vehicle takes on quite a different appearance carrying a jazz band in support of Edinburgh University Rag Week. Rag Week is still going strong and was recently described by a participant as 'a mad seven days of collecting, events and partying, climaxing with the floats parade on Princes Street'.

This aerial view shows Dalry Road running diagonally across the bottom left-hand corner and Dundee Street running diagonally across the top right of the picture. Between the two roads is the Caledonian Railway line (now the route of the West Approach Road) out of Princes Street station. To the left of the main track is Dalry station on the branch line to Granton. Pedestrian access to the station was from the 'subway' between Dundee Street and the south end of Orwell Terrace, which is still a right of way although the station was demolished many years ago. To the left of Dalry station is a siding giving access to Colin Macandrew & Partners' yard and the premises of Alexander Mather & Sons, engineers, of Orwell Terrace. Dalry Cemetery can be seen in the bottom right-hand corner of the photograph.

The Orwell Works of Alexander Mather & Son in Orwell Terrace was a hive of activity with lathes, an overhead gantry crane and a light railway all competing for space when this photograph was taken in 1921. The main contracts at Fountainbridge and later at Orwell Terrace were for the construction and supply of oatmeal and barley milling machines, conveyor and elevator equipment, cutting and stacking machines for paper mills, and printing ink manufacturing plant. Mather's main customers were A. & R. Scott (makers of porridge oats), Imperial Chemical Industries, Distillers Company Ltd., Scottish Malt Distillers, A. B. Fleming & Co., and a host of firms in Australia, New Zealand, South Africa, Norway and Sweden.

Another early view of Mather's extensive premises in Orwell Terrace showing how the various lathes and other metalworking machinery were powered by a system of overhead belts and pulleys from a single power unit, probably located away from the main shop floor. Each piece of machinery was fitted with a long lever which enabled the operator to stop his machine by moving the power belt from the moving pulley wheel to an idle one.

Among the most difficult items to manoeuvre out of Mather's Orwell Works and onto the adjacent railway track were the girders for the Murrayfield Bridge which were produced for the Caledonian Railway in 1900. This photograph shows the girders loaded onto at least ten waggons next to Dalry station, ready for the journey. The distinctive awning, projecting from the station building, can be seen in the top left-hand corner of the picture.

Out of the apparent confusion of the shop floor came order and dependability. One of the many finished products, often designated for export, was this milling machine constructed by Mather's in 1893 when the firm was still at Fountainbridge.

In 1870, long before the internal combustion engine became commonplace, Mather's designed and built a steam-powered tractor which was on show at the International Exhibition of Industry, Science and Art held in the East Meadows in the summer of 1886. It was a short, stocky, three-wheeled vehicle with massive rear wheels supporting the steam boiler and funnel. Two men were required to operate it: the driver sat perched at the front in an open cab, while a second person was stationed on a projecting platform at the back, presumably to stoke the boiler. ('Tractor' in this sense means a vehicle designed to tow heavy loads.)

In the opening years of the twentieth century Mather's entered the new and challenging age of the motor car. As well as being appointed agents for Clement delivery vans, they announced in their advertising material that 'almost every make of car in general use in the country has passed through the works, in many cases having been entirely rebuilt'. The business was sufficiently prosperous to warrant the opening of a car showroom in 1906 at 79–81 Shandwick Place, and to have a stand at the Kelvin Hall Motor Show in the following years.

This picture of Mather's garage facilities is entitled 'View in South Garage, Orwell Terrace, showing Repair Pits and part of Workshop'.

This photograph shows Prince George visiting the carving shop of Scott Morton & Co., cabinetmakers, in Murieston Road in 1933. William Stewart Morton (son of the founder William Scott Morton) is on the extreme left with Bob Young, foreman carver, on the right. The firm was principally involved in the design and manufacture of furniture, but also set up a separate company, the Tynecastle Company, which made a wide range of plaster mouldings and embossed canvas wallcoverings. From 1890 to 1916 materials for the interiors of private houses, designed by several eminent Scottish architects, formed a large part of Scott Morton's work. These included carvings, panelling, library shelves, staircases and furniture. The lengthy list of properties concerned, covering many parts of the country, included: No. 6 Heriot Row, Edinburgh, for Alexander Maitland, by Sir Robert Lorimer; Harmeny, Balerno, for W. J. Younger, also by Lorimer; and the restoration of Falkland Palace for the Marquess of Bute, by John Kinross. Scott Morton also worked on the interior of the National Library of Scotland on George IV Bridge, along with Colin Macandrew & Partners, also of Dalry, who built the stonework. This project, undertaken in the mid-1950s, was probably one of Scott Morton's last big contracts. In the 1960s the firm saw considerable reduction in orders for high-grade decorative interiors, as a result of which it closed in 1966.

The North British Rubber Company Ltd. was established in 1856 by Henry Lee Norris, who brought four employees, Louise Dixon, Sophia Terry, Hannah Dixon and Walter P. Dunn to Edinburgh from the USA to start the business. The adventurous foursome sailed to Scotland in the windjammer *Harmonia* with machinery valued at £370 to begin the manufacture of boots and shoes in what had been Castle Silk Mills on the north bank of the Union Canal in Edinburgh. It was not long before the business was well established, eventually extending its range of products beyond footwear to include motor car tyres, conveyor belts, combs, golf balls, hot water bottles and rubber flooring. At its peak the firm employed 9,000 workers, many of them in the vulcanite department (seen here in 1907) with its distinctive square, brick-built water tower in the foreground. This part of the works had previously been a separate entity, the Scottish Vulcanite Company, but was absorbed into the North British Rubber Company in the early twentieth century.

The cash department of the North British Rubber Company at Castle Mills. The factory had a large number of suppliers and an even greater number of sales outlets throughout the United Kingdom and abroad. It was here that the staff monitored the progress, or lack of progress, in establishing new lines – sometimes to a sceptical public. Even in the 1950s, when the company introduced the Green Hunter and Royal Hunter wellington boots, uptake was slow, with an order for a few dozen pairs regarded as reasonably satisfactory.

An operative washing rubber in the hot, steamy atmosphere of Castle Mills. Among the North British Rubber Company's many products were groundsheets and anti-gas curtains for the use of the British Army and the public during both World Wars. Over a million trench boots were made for soldiers at the front, and miles and miles of hose was produced for pumping out the water-filled trenches. During the Second World War the company had a Government contract with the War Office to manufacture a camouflage material for the use of British troops in Europe. The material was successfully designed by Ursula Davidson of Edinburgh who had already earned herself a considerable reputation as an interior designer. Ms Davidson died at the age of 89 in 2001. Rubber is obtained from latex, a milky liquid exuded by certain plants, particularly *Hevea brasiliensis*, a native of Brazil as the name suggests. Until around 1900 most of the world's rubber was grown wild in the Amazon, but by 1914 a much greater quantity was being produced in controlled plantations. Between 1900 and 1940 the use of rubber throughout the world increased phenomenally mainly to meet the demand for motor car tyres. When the supply of natural rubber was interrupted during the Second World War, synthetic rubber was introduced. This was often found easier to modify for specific purposes, for example to make it fire or oil resistant.

Facing page: It has not been possible to ascertain precisely what processes are being undertaken by each of the operatives working this complicated machine for the production of motor car tyres. As early as 1870 – more than twenty years before the introduction of the pneumatic tyre – R. W. Thomson introduced his 'road steamer' wheels which were covered with rims of vulcanised rubber made by the North British Rubber Co. The company had a long history of producing motor car accessories, some of which created unusual problems for the workforce. In the late 1960s, the North British Rubber Co. was forced to defend itself against accusations of unfairness for introducing a requirement that all applicants for a specific department had to be right-handed. This was to facilitate the efficient production of fascia crash pads for car dashboards. The company explained that the assembly line required that everyone be 'same-handed', and that there were many left-handed employees in other departments.

A machine for manufacturing motor car tyres at the North British Rubber Company's works.

This photograph shows George F. Simpson of Edinburgh sitting in the 'baby' Austin 7, registration SF 9917, which he succeeded in driving to the top of Ben Nevis on 6 October 1928 – helped to a considerable degree by Clincher tyres, made by the North British Rubber Company and prominently on display here. Stunts such as this generated excellent publicity for the makers of both the car and its tyres. The first car to reach the summit of Ben Nevis was a Ford, driven by Henry Alexander in 1911.

This undated photograph almost certainly shows an advertising venture by the North British Rubber Company at the Braid Hills Golf Course. The barrage-type balloon carries the advertisement 'Clincher Cross Golf Balls' – these were made by the company from around 1913. The two smaller balloons reproduce the effect of the 'square dimple' of the Clincher golf ball. Decorated with advertising slogans, these round balloons were made, complete with packing box, reels, cords and anchorage, for customers including the *Isle of Man Times*, and were also used to advertise Clincher Tyres – 'For Comfort and Long Mileage'. A reel and box can be seen immediately below the right-hand balloon. The intricacies of making golf balls at the North British Rubber Co. was the subject of a lengthy article in *The Scotsman* in 1949, which revealed that over 24,000 balls were manufactured each week. Originally the centre of the balls consisted of a small balloon filled with paste, but this was later replaced by a hard rubber sphere with non-solidifying oil in the centre. Three hundred yards of half-inch wide rubber was wound round the sphere – by hand – to make each ball. Also added by hand were the green, blue, red or black spots – a task which attracted the very latest technology of the day – a bent pin and a piece of wood! The wood acted as a rudimentary handle and the head of the pin, in the hands of an experienced operative, gave the exact size of blob. A test catapulting machine was used at the Edinburgh University athletics ground at Craiglockhart. Not only did the company's employees make golf balls, but they also used them as members of the Weba Golf Club founded by North British Rubber Company employees around 1886. It was sometimes said that the name 'Weba' was a contraction of 'wee ba' ', but in fact it was taken from the initials of a previous general manager, W. E. Bartlett. Also in the picture, on the extreme left, is an advertisement for 'The Challenger Golf Ball' which was made by rival manufacturer J. P. Cochrane & Co. Ltd. of Leith from 1917.

Infirmary pageants were an annual event that most large employers in Edinburgh took part in, especially in the 1920s and 1930s. This float is by the boot and shoe department of the North British Rubber Company and carries several slogans advertising their products. 'For summer sand or winters snow, North British shoes are all the go', and 'Shoe-r in Yer Siller' to encourage the crowd to throw in more than just their coppers. On the cab door is a poster depicting an infant holding a bucket bearing the words 'for a good cause', below which is the caption 'Give – and keep smiling till you've nothing in your pockets – just like me'.

This photograph of shopfronts at Nos. 22, 24 and 26 Dalry Road is difficult to date. For several years around 1900 No. 24 was occupied by Mrs Allan as a dairy, and No. 26 was occupied by Leonard Frank, butcher. However, during the same period of occupancy No. 22 appears to have been used by the photographer John Drummond, but it is not his name which appears on the signage here.

The interior of the spirit store at the Caledonian Distillery at Distillery Lane near Haymarket. The Caledonian was built by Graham Menzies & Co. who owned Sunbury Distillery near the Dean village. It opened in 1855, making it one of the first firms to move into the Dalry area which, at that time, was a greenfield site with ample space for expansion. However, there were other factors which influenced the decision to locate at Dalry. The site lay between the lines of the Caledonian Railway and the Edinburgh & Glasgow Railway, both of which provided branch lines which led into the works. In addition, the Union Canal was relatively close, providing a gravity-fed supply of water for cooling which was carried in an underground pipe nearly a mile long. Although the Caledonian moved to Dalry in 1855 to gain the advantage of greater space, the passage of time removed that asset completely, forcing the owners, United Distillers, to close the complex and relocate in 1987. Parts of the remaining buildings, including the tall chimney, have since been listed and are now surrounded by modern flats.

The engine seen here being coaled up at Dalry is believed to be No. 905, one of five magnificent 4-6-0 locomotives in the 903 Class, designed by the Caledonian's locomotive superintendent J. F. McIntosh in 1906. When this engine came into service the Caledonian Railway was already almost 60 years old. A west coast route from London to Scotland was first considered in 1836 by the Grand Junction Railway but it was not until 1844 that a proposal was approved to extend the line from Carstairs northwards, providing separate branches serving Glasgow and Edinburgh. The new Caledonian Railway line was opened between Carlisle and Beattock on 10 September 1847, finally opening to Edinburgh on 15 February 1848. The line ran westwards through the city from Lothian Road, along what is now the West Approach Road, under Morrison Street and Dundee Street to stations at Merchiston and Slateford. The main station at the West End of Princes Street was completed in 1894 (after several problems with earlier stations on the same site) and was incorporated into the grand Caledonian Hotel in 1903. The station closed in 1965.

This line of open-topped cable cars, apparently crammed with male passengers only, was photographed in Dalry Road c.1920, a few hundred yards west of the Haymarket road junction. The first car has a destination board 'Portobello for Joppa' and an advertisement for Nubolic soap; the second car is bound for Pilrig and advertises Zebra polish. The picture was probably taken on a Saturday afternoon when Hearts were playing at home at Tynecastle. Cable cars were first introduced to Edinburgh in 1893 when Edinburgh Corporation secured powers to convert the existing horse tramways to mechanised operation. The cars were hauled along the road by a moving cable, running in a slot below the level of the road surface between the rails. It was a cumbersome system which was prone to frequent breakdown.

A much more sophisticated transport system, using electric tramcars, was introduced to replace the cable cars. Electric trams were running in Musselburgh in 1904, Leith in 1905, and along a short line from Ardmillan to Slateford in 1910, but it was not until 1919 that Edinburgh decided on complete conversion to electric power. Implementation was delayed whilst a new electricity generating station was built at Portobello with sub-stations throughout the city. This photograph shows car No. 184 on service 4 to Slateford travelling westwards on Dalry Road. The driver is about to turn to his left, past the policeman on points duty, and into Ardmillan Terrace. Dalry Cemetery can be seen on the right behind the high wall. The photograph was taken in May 1953 and the last electric tram in Edinburgh ran on 16 November 1956.

The City Architect, Robert Morham, first submitted his plans for the erection of 'public baths and washhouses' in Dalry in 1893. These were completed in 1895 on the south side of Caledonian Crescent. The main pool measured 75 by 35 feet and varied in depth from 3 feet to 6 feet 3 inches. There was also a small shallow pool in which prospective bathers were expected to dally, in the interests of hygiene, before entering the main pool. At pool level there were changing rooms on the north side for ladies and a similar arrangement on the south side for men. Hot, private baths, located around the balcony, were very popular with local people, many of whom lived in houses which did not have baths fitted. Patrons could chose between first class at 1/3d., and second class at 9d., both of which lasted for half an hour. First-class patrons had the luxury of unlimited hot water, whereas those opting for second class had to make do with the bath being filled once only. The private baths were discontinued in 1980. In 1991 Dalry Baths were closed for repair and extensive modernisation; they were reopened as Dalry Swim Centre on 12 February 1993 by Lord Provost Norman Irons.

The staff of Dalry Baths on the entrance steps on the south side of Caledonian Crescent in 1905, with superintendent Baillie (father of Charlie Baillie, the Olympic swimmer) in the centre. The poster in the background announces an Annual Gala at Dalry Baths on Friday 14 October by the Edinburgh Swimming Club and Humane Society. Mr Baillie and his family lived in a small flat incorporated into the west side of the baths complex. The apparently large staff shown in the picture was probably required because of the high number of private baths in operation. These were labour-intensive to maintain and operate.

Members of the Grove Swimming Club photographed in 1922 on an outing, possibly to Portobello, with Charlie Baillie, the Olympic swimmer, on the extreme left of the picture. For many years Dalry Baths have been the home of the Grove Swimming Club. The exact date of the club's founding is unknown but it was probably inaugurated in 1901 under its full name, Grove Swimming Club and Humane Society. Its first patron was the Marquis of Linlithgow.

This very historic photograph shows British sportsmen and women at the 1924 Paris Olympic Games. On the left in the back row is Charlie Baillie, who was a member of Grove Swimming Club. Charlie, born in 1902, was Scottish champion in the 50 and 100 yards championships every year from 1920 to 1926. He also won several English championships when he later moved to Oldham. The highlight of his career was, however, the 1924 Paris Olympics, the games in which Eric Liddell, of *Chariots of Fire* fame, also competed. Eric Liddell appears at the right-hand end of the middle row in this picture.

A hostelry has stood on the site of the present Ryrie's Bar at Haymarket from time immemorial. It was the Haymarket Inn from at least as early as 1862 and the premises were remodelled for Messrs. Ryrie & Co. in 1906.

Staff and customers at Nisbet's Bar, Dalry Road, in the 1920s. In the back row, second from the left is F. H. Kumerer, the pork butcher, whose shop was at 26 Dalry Road; fourth from the left is Tom Scott Snr., engine driver with the North British Railway Co. The gentleman with the hat, third from the right, is Sam Drennan, the boot repairer.

John McBain the fruiterer, ready for his rounds, photographed at Murieston Lane outside the timber yard of Scott Morton the cabinetmakers.

Dairyman James Morren delivered milk daily in the Dalry area to customers who brought their own jugs out to the cart to be filled from one of the large containers.

Cathcart Place was built in the late 1870s but the derivation of the name remains unknown. The photograph is taken looking south-east towards Dalry Parish Church on the corner of Dalry Road.

Murieston Crescent in the first decade of the twentieth century. This picture postcard was franked at 1.30 p.m. on 21 April 1906 and sent to Durham. The sender put a cross on the front of the card and referred to it in her message: 'I've put an x for our parlour windows – it's a good view'. On the extreme left of the picture is the railway bridge carrying the Wester Dalry branch line of the Caledonian Railway under the main line at the higher level.

Dalry Road looking eastwards (towards the city centre) near the junction with Murieston Crescent c.1919, with the railway bridge and Dalry Parish Church in the background. The lamp standard on the left of the picture has a sign, high up, reading 'CARS STOP' and referring to the cable car system. Lower down is a small, almost indecipherable sign which looks very similar to those which were fixed to many cable car or tram car stops and read: 'PLEASE DO NOT SPIT ON THE PAVEMENT'. Young boys were not averse to climbing lamp standards and removing the letter 'P' from the fourth word. In mock defiance they would then sit on the pavement nearby pointing up to the sign in the hope of attracting some hard-earned disapproval from passers-by. Starting from the corner shop and working towards the bridge, the traders include: No. 230, James Dryden, grocer & provision merchant; No. 228, D. Small, tobacconist; No. 226, cycle repair shop; No. 224, unknown; and No. 222, Miss C. W. Tod, dairy.

Looking up Ardmillan Terrace from its junction with Dalry Road and Gorgie Road in the days of the isolated electric tramway route from here to Slateford, which was in operation between June 1910 and October 1920. Cars on this electric section were hauled out from Shrubhill to Ardmillan on a daily basis and unhitched to the west of the Ardmillan junction, from where they could make a right turn into Ardmillan Terrace to begin the route. The track in the foreground belongs to the cable car system which ran from the city centre to Saughton, while that in Ardmillan Terrace itself is part of the electrified route. The small row of shops at the foot of the terrace are, from left to right: No. 1, Bank of Scotland; No. 2, David Brown, cabinetmaker and upholsterer; No. 3, Mrs Wilson, stationer and post office (with the post box outside); No. 5, David Penman, furniture dealers, with some items for sale out on the pavement.

This aerial view shows the Union Canal as a dark, broad strip running diagonally right from the centre of the lower edge of the picture. To the left of the canal, and running parallel to it, is Dundee Street / Fountainbridge. Also to the left of the canal, on the bank between the two bridges, is the main part of the extensive premises of the North British Rubber Co. Ltd. Fountain House, marking the south entrance to the original Dalry estate and illustrated on page 7, is circled. This is one of the few surviving pictures to show the house and its immediate surroundings shortly before its demolition in 1935.

In 1911 Miss Robertson, a piano teacher who lived in Harrison Road, retired early to look after her own children. However, she decided to have a retirement picnic to which all her former pupils were invited, many of whom lived in Gorgie or Dalry. The group, with Miss Robertson fourth from the left in the back row, is seen here at Cramond.

During the 1920s the Royal Infirmary of Edinburgh Pageant was an important social occasion which had the serious task of raising money for the hospital under the slogan 'In Health – Remember the Sick'. In 1923 the infirmary issued some facts and figures to encourage the public to contribute more money. For the year to 1 October 1922, the infirmary's expenditure was £119,759 against an income of £99,171, making a deficit of £20,588 which was met from legacies received. The photograph shows the children and young adults of Dalry on their float outside No. 3 Caledonian Crescent. Wm. McEwan & Co. Ltd., the brewers, supplied the lorry and the procession went along Princes Street, Lothian Road and the streets of the Old Town.

The Scott family were brought up in a small flat at 6 Caledonian Crescent in the early 1920s. Tom Scott Snr. (see page 38) was an engine driver with the North British Railway and he and his wife, Williamina, brought up a large family of four sons and three daughters. From left to right are: Bill Scott outside 6 Caledonian Crescent, c.1927; Mary (Molly) Scott with the family pet, Ruf, outside St Bride's Parish Church in Orwell Terrace; and Tom Scott, also with Ruf, in Roseburn Park.